The Standard Publishing Company, Cincinnati, Ohio.
A division of Standex International Corporation.
© 1992 by The Standard Publishing Company
Printed in the United States of America
99 98 97 96 95 94 93 92   5 4 3 2 1

Library of Congress Cataloging-in-Publication Data
Stortz, Diane M.
Zaccheus meets Jesus : Luke 19:1-10 /
retold by Diane Stortz ; illustrated by Todd Fagan.
ISBN O-87403-958-4
Library of Congress Catalog Card Number 91-46811

Zaccheus
Meets Jesus

Luke 19:1-10 retold by
Diane Stortz

illustrated by Todd Fagan

STANDARD
PUBLISHING

"When Jesus came to that place,
he looked up and saw
Zaccheus in the tree."

Luke 19:5

Zaccheus, the tax collector,

was a rich man,

a short man,
a curious man
who wanted
to see Jesus.

Because even though Zaccheus
was very rich,
he was also very lonely.

Sometimes tax collectors cheated.
They took too much tax from people,
and they kept the extra money for themselves.

No one likes to be cheated,
so Zaccheus didn't have many friends.

But Zaccheus had heard about someone special,
a man named Jesus
who taught about God's love.
Zaccheus wanted to meet Jesus
and talk to Him about God.

"Maybe Jesus would be my friend,"
Zaccheus thought.

One day Zaccheus heard a shout.

"Jesus is coming!" called mothers and fathers and boys and girls.

Everyone was running to the side of the road to see Jesus as He passed by.

Zaccheus ran too.
But because he was so short,

he couldn't see over the heads
of the people in the crowd.

And no one would let him through
to the front of the line.

So Zaccheus ran to a tree
by the side of the road
and quickly climbed up into its branches.

He climbed from branch to branch,

"At my house?" thought Zaccheus. "No one has ever wanted to come to my house!"

Zaccheus climbed down
in a hurry
and took Jesus home
for dinner.
The people of Jericho
started to whine.

"Look at that!" they said.
"Jesus has gone
to eat with Zaccheus.

Everyone knows
about the bad things
Zaccheus has done."
But Zaccheus
didn't hear them.
He was too busy listening
to Jesus, his new friend.

He kept listening, all through dinner,

and he decided
to stop cheating people
and start doing right.

"I'm going to give half of everything
I have to the poor,"
Zaccheus told Jesus.
"And if I have cheated anyone,
I'll pay him back four times as much."

Jesus was pleased.

Now Zaccheus was a rich man,

a short man,

and a happy man
because he had met Jesus
and decided to do right!